21

Keys For A Better Marriage

By Don and Phaedra Johnson

ISBN 979-8-9889779-0-2 (paperback)

Printed in USA

First Edition

Contents

Keys and strategies to build
and maintain a happier,
healthier marriage.

Introduction

In today's fast-paced world, maintaining a healthy and fulfilling marriage requires effort and dedication. This book presents 21 practical and insightful KEYS and strategies to build and maintain a happier, healthier marriage. Keep in mind, marriage is a journey filled with love, joy and growth. But it also requires effort, commitment and continuous nurturing. As you go throughout your day you are faced with external pressures and distractions that can easily strain your relationship. Therefore, it is essential to prioritize the health and well-being of your marriage.

Whether you are newlyweds embarking on this lifelong partnership, you've been married for years and seek to strengthen your bond, you're looking for ways to rebuild and reignite the spark in your marriage, you're engaged or you're dating and have a desire to be married, this book will provide you with KEYS that contain valuable insights, practical tips and proven strategies for creat-ing a fulfilling and harmonious marriage.

Keep in mind every marriage is unique, and there is no one-size-fits-all approach. So we will offer a range of keys and strategies that you can adapt to fit your own unique circumstances, values, and goals. Remember, a healthy marriage is not about perfection or the absence of challenges. It is about cultivating a deep sense of love, respect, and partnership, even in the face of difficulties. It requires open communication, mutual understand-ing, and a commitment to growth as individuals and as a couple.

Get ready to embark on this transformative journey towards a stronger, happier, and more resilient marriage. Let the KEYS and strategies outlined in these pages unlock the doors to a fulfilling marriage. Your commitment to building and maintaining a healthy marriage will not only benefit you and your spouse, but will also create a positive ripple effect that extends to your families, communities, and future generations. Let's begin this Amazing adventure together.

Chapter 1
Effective Communication

*"Learn to communicate openly,
honestly, and respectfully."*

E ffective communication is vital for building a healthy and thriving marriage. It allows couples to express their thoughts, needs, and emotions while fostering understanding and connection. In this chapter, we will explore keys and strategies of effective communication that can help you navigate challenges, resolve conflicts, and deepen your bond as a couple.

1.1 Open and Honest Communication:

Openness and honesty form the foundation of effective communication. It also creates a safe space where both of you feel comfortable expressing yourselves without fear of judgment or reprisal.

Practice these **KEYS**:

- Encourage open dialogue by actively listening to your spouse's thoughts and feelings.

- Share your own thoughts, needs, and emotions with honesty and vulnerability.

- Be receptive to feedback and willing to address any concerns raised by your spouse.

- Foster an environment where difficult conversations can occur without defensiveness.

1.2 Active Listening:

Active listening is a crucial aspect of effective communication. It demonstrates respect, empathy, and a genuine interest in understanding your spouse. This means giving your spouse your full attention and focusing on understanding their message without interrupting or formulating a response in your mind.

Practice these **KEYS**:

- Give your full attention to your spouse, maintaining eye contact and non-verbal engagement.

- Avoid interrupting or planning your response while your spouse is speaking.

- Ask clarifying questions to ensure you understand their perspective accurately.

- Eliminate distractions and create a conducive environment for open conversation.

- Summarize or paraphrase what your spouse has said to show that you have actively listened.

- Ask yourself this question: Are you really listening or are you just waiting your turn to talk.

1.3 Express Yourself Clearly:

Communication is a two-way street and it is equally important to express yourself clearly and effectively.

Practice these **KEYS**:

- Use "I" statements to express your feelings and thoughts without blaming or criticizing your spouse.

- Be specific about your needs, desires, and concerns.

- Use a calm and non-confrontational tone to avoid escalating tensions.

- Take responsibility for your own emotions and reactions.

1.4 Non-Verbal Communication:

Non-verbal cues can significantly impact communication. Pay attention to your body language, tone of voice, facial expressions and gestures to ensure they align with the message you're trying to convey.

*Practice these **KEYS**:*

- Maintain open body language, such as facing your spouse, uncrossing your arms, and nodding to show understanding.

- Use facial expressions and gestures to convey empathy, interest, and understanding.

- Match your tone of voice with the intended message, avoiding harsh or dismissive tones.

- Be aware of your spouse's non-verbal cues, as they can offer insights into their emotions.

- Offer physical affection, such as hugs or hand-holding, to reinforce feelings of love and support.

1.5 Respectful Language:

The choice of words and tone can greatly influence the effectiveness of your communication. Practice using respectful language to foster healthy dialogue.

Practice these **KEYS:**

- Speak with kindness and avoid using derogatory or demeaning language.

- Use "I" statements to express your feelings and needs without blaming or accusing.

- Focus on the specific behavior or situation at hand, rather than attacking your spouse's character.

- Keep a calm tone during challenging or emotional conversations.

1.6 Timing and Context:

Choosing the right time and context for important conversations can significantly impact the outcome.

Practice these **KEYS:**

- Pick a time when both you and your spouse are calm and receptive.

- Find a private and quiet space where you can talk without distractions.

- Avoid discussing sensitive topics when either of you are tired or stressed.

1.7 Empathy and Understanding:

Cultivating empathy and understanding in your communication can help bridge gaps and strengthen your connection as a couple.

Practice these **KEYS:**

- Put yourself in your spouse's shoes and strive to understand their perspective.

- Validate their emotions and experiences, even if you don't necessarily agree with them.

- Respond with empathy and compassion, demonstrating that you value and acknowledge their feelings.

- Practice active curiosity, seeking to learn more about your spouse's thoughts, values, and experiences.

1.8 Respectful Disagreements:

It is unrealistic to expect complete agreement all the time. Learn how to respectfully disagree and navigate differing opinions.

Practice these **KEYS:**

- Avoid personal attacks and focus on the issue at hand.

- Raising your voice doesn't make your point more believable.

- Seek to understand your spouse's viewpoint and be open to changing your own perspective.

- Look for win-win solutions that honor both of your needs and values.

1.9 Provide Validation:

Providing feedback and validation is essential for effective communication.

Practice these **KEYS**:

- Acknowledge your spouse's efforts, ideas and feelings.
- Validate their emotions and show empathy even if you don't fully agree.
- Celebrate successes and express appreciation for their contributions.

1.10 Regular Check-Ins and Feedback:

Regularly checking in with each other and providing feedback is crucial for maintaining open lines of communication.

Practice these **KEYS**:

- Schedule regular time to discuss your relationship, goals and challenges.
- Express appreciation for positive communication moments and efforts.
- Celebrate and acknowledge growth in your communication skills as a couple.
- Offer constructive feedback using gentle and positive language.

Effective communication is a skill that can be developed and refined over time. A critical key to opening these doors are making sure your filter is clean. In your home there is a filter that's designed to keep dust and dirt particles out of your house. If that filter isn't cleaned it can cause your aller-gies to flare up. There is also a filter in your car that needs to be changed. If it's not cleaned, the engine will shut down. By practicing active listen-ing, expressing yourself clearly, being respectful during disagreements and offering feedback and validation, you can create an environment of open and honest communication in your marriage. Re-member, communication is a continuous process. So be sure to make it a priority to regularly check in with each other and fine-tune your communi-cation skills in an effort to nurture a strong and lasting bond.

Chapter 2
Practicing Empathy

"Put yourself in your spouse's shoes and strive to understand their perspective."

E mpathy is a powerful tool that allows us to understand and connect with our spouse on a deeper level. It involves putting ourselves in their shoes, acknowledging their emotions and responding with compassion and understanding. In this chapter, we will explore the importance of empathy in a marriage and discuss practical KEYS to cultivate and practice empathy in your relationship.

2.1 Understanding Emotions:

Empathy begins with recognizing and understanding your spouse's emotions. This requires attentive listening and genuine interest in their feelings.

Practice these **KEYS**:

- Pay attention to your spouse's verbal and non-verbal cues to gauge their emotional state.

- Ask open-ended questions to encourage them to express their emotions.

- Reflect on their emotions to show that you truly comprehend their experiences.

2.2 Active Listening:

Active listening is an integral part of empathy. When your spouse shares their thoughts and feelings, give them your undivided attention.

Practice these **KEYS**:

- Maintain eye contact and focus on what they are saying.

- Avoid interrupting or formulating responses in your mind.

- Use verbal and non-verbal cues to show that you are fully engaged.

- Paraphrase and summarize their words to ensure you understand their perspective.

2.3 Perspective:

Empathy involves stepping into your spouse's shoes and seeing the world from their viewpoint.

Practice these **KEYS**:

- Imagining how you would feel if you were in their situation.

- Considering their background, experiences and personal history.

- Setting aside judgment or preconceived notions.

- Being open to understanding their unique perspective.

2.4 Validating Emotions:

Validation is an essential aspect of empathy. It communicates acceptance and understanding to your spouse.

Practice these **KEYS**:

- Acknowledge and accept your spouse's emotions without judgment.

- Express empathy and understanding through verbal affirmations like "I understand how you feel" or "That must be challenging for you."

- Validate their emotions, even if you don't fully agree or share the same feelings.

- Offer reassurance and support to let them know they are not alone in their experiences.

2.5 Emotional Support:

Empathy involves providing emotional support to your spouse.

Practice these **KEYS**:

- Be present and available when your spouse needs to talk or seek comfort.

- Offer a listening ear, a shoulder to lean on, or a comforting hug.

- Avoid minimizing or dismissing their feelings, even if you don't fully comprehend or relate to their emotions.

- Provide words of encouragement and reassurance during challenging times.

2.6 Empathy in Conflict Resolution:

Empathy plays a vital role in resolving conflicts constructively.

Practice these **KEYS**:

- Listen actively to your spouse's perspective, seeking to understand their underlying emotions and concerns.

- Acknowledge and validate their feelings and needs.

- Express your understanding of their point of view before presenting your own.

- Look for common ground and mutually beneficial solutions.

- Practice compromise and strive for Win-Win outcomes.

2.7 Cultivating Empathy:

Cultivating empathy is an ongoing process. Here are some strategies to develop and strengthen empathy in your marriage.

Practice these **KEYS**:

- Practice self-reflection and emotional awareness to better understand your own emotions and reactions.

- Engage in activities that promote empathy, such as volunteering together or engaging in meaningful conversations about others' experiences.

- Encourage open and honest communication in your marriage, creating a safe space for sharing emotions and vulnerabilities.

- Regularly check in with your spouse about their emotional well-being and actively listen to their concerns.

Empathy is a transformative force that fosters deeper emotional connection and understanding in your marriage. By understanding emotions, actively listening, taking perspectives, validating feelings, providing emotional support, incorporating empathy into conflict resolution and continuously cultivating empathy, you can create a nurturing and empathetic environment in your relationship. Remember, empathy requires practice and intentionality, but the rewards in your marriage are immeasurable.

Chapter 3
Showing Appreciation

"Regularly express gratitude for your spouse's efforts, support and love."

Appreciation is a powerful and often underestimated aspect of a healthy and thriving marriage. It involves expressing gratitude and recognition for your spouse's contributions, love and support. In this chapter, we will explore the importance of showing appreciation in your marriage and discuss practical keys to incorporate this essential element into your relationship.

3.1 The Power of Appreciation:

Appreciation serves as a foundation for fostering love, connection and happiness in your marriage. It reinforc-es positive behavior, boosts self-esteem and strength-ens the emotional bond between you and your spouse. Recognizing the value of appreciation sets the stage for creating a nurturing and supportive relationship.

Practice these **KEYS**:

- Acknowledge their daily contributions, such as household chores, parenting or financial respon-sibilities.

- Recognize their emotional support, understanding and care.

- Appreciate their personal growth and efforts to strengthen the relationship.

3.2 Express Gratitude:

Verbal expressions of gratitude can have a profound impact on your spouse's well-being and the overall atmosphere of your marriage.

Practice these **KEYS**:

- Regularly verbalize your appreciation by saying "Thank You" for both small and significant gestures.

- Be specific about what you are grateful for by highlighting the actions, strengths or qualities you admire in your spouse.

- Use positive and encouraging language to convey your appreciation.

- Create a routine of sharing your appreciation by dedicating a few minutes each day to express what you appreciate about each other.

3.3 Thoughtful Gestures:

Thoughtful gestures can make a significant impact on your spouse's feelings of appreciation and love.

Practice these **KEYS**:

- Surprise them with small gifts or tokens of affection that hold personal meaning.

- Plan surprises or special occasions to celebrate milestones and achievements.

- Write heartfelt notes or letters expressing your appreciation for their love, support and efforts.

- Anticipate their needs and show care through small acts like preparing their favorite snack or beverage.

3.6 Public Acknowledgment:

Publicly acknowledging your spouse's value and contributions can boost their self-esteem and strengthen your bond.

Practice these **KEYS**:

- Praise and express your appreciation for your spouse in front of family and friends.

- Share your spouse's achievements and efforts on social media or during public gatherings.

- Celebrate their successes and milestones publicly, highlighting their dedication and hard work.

3.7 Compliments and Affection:

Offering sincere compliments and affectionate gestures can convey your appreciation effectively.

Practice these **KEYS**:

- Compliment your spouse on their appearance, character traits, skills or efforts.

- Show physical affection through hugs, kisses, hand-holding or cuddling to reinforce feelings of love and connection.

- Be mindful of non-verbal cues, such as smiling or maintaining eye contact, to communicate warmth and appreciation.

Showing appreciation is a transformative practice that can enrich your marriage. By recognizing and valuing your spouse's contributions, expressing gratitude through words and actions, offering thoughtful gestures, publicly acknowledging their worth and cultivating a culture of appreciation, you can create a foundation of love and gratitude that strengthens your bond and fosters a joyful and fulfilling relationship. Embrace the power of appreciation and watch your relationship thrive.

Chapter 4
Emotional Intimacy

*"Put the time in, beautiful grass takes a lot of work.
Unless it's turf."*

E motional intimacy forms the foundation of a deep and fulfilling marriage. It is the bond that connects you and your spouse on an emotional level, fostering trust, vulnerability, and a sense of shared understanding. In this chapter, we will explore the importance of nurturing emotional intimacy in your marriage and provide practical strategies to cultivate and strengthen this essential aspect of your relationship.

4.1 Creating a Safe Space

To nurture emotional intimacy, it is crucial to create a safe and supportive non-judgmental environment where both you and your spouse feel comfortable expressing your thoughts, feelings, and vulnerabilities.

Practice these **KEYS**:

- Create a safe space for open and honest communication, where you and your spouse feel comfortable expressing your thoughts and feelings without fear of criticism or rejection.

- Listen attentively to your spouse's words and validate their emotions without criticism or defensiveness.

- Validate and affirm your spouse's experiences, showing empathy and understanding.

- Be trustworthy and maintain confidentiality, ensuring that sensitive information or vulnerabilities are treated with utmost respect.

4.2 Sharing Feelings and Experiences:

Sharing your feelings and experiences is a powerful way to deepen emotional intimacy.

Practice these **KEYS**:

- Initiate conversations about your emotions, fears, dreams, and desires.

- Be vulnerable and open about your own experiences, allowing your spouse to understand you on a deeper level.

- Encourage your spouse to share their thoughts and emotions, creating an atmosphere of mutual trust and support.

- Practice active listening and demonstrate genuine interest in their experiences.

4.3 Deepening Emotional Connection:

Cultivating emotional intimacy requires intentional efforts to deepen your emotional connection.

Practice these **KEYS**:

- Engage in activities that promote emotional bonding, such as having deep conversations, sharing memories, or engaging in shared hobbies.
- Prioritize quality time together, free from distractions, to nurture a sense of emotional closeness.
- Express affection, both verbally and physically, to reinforce your emotional connection.
- Continuously learn about your spouse's evolving needs, dreams, and desires to foster ongoing emotional connection.

4.4 Emotional Support:

Emotional intimacy involves being there for your spouse during both joyful and challenging times.

Practice these **KEYS**:

- Showing genuine interest in their feelings, concerns, and experiences.
- Offer a shoulder to lean on and lend a listening ear during times of stress or difficulty.
- Offering encouragement, reassurance, and affirmation to help them navigate difficult situations.
- Being a source of comfort and understanding during times of stress or sadness.

4.5 Make It A Priority:

Nurturing emotional intimacy requires ongoing effort and attention.

Practice these **KEYS**:

- Establish consistent time to connect, such as sharing meals together, engaging in daily check-ins, or practicing gratitude together.

- Make time for shared experiences and create opportunities for emotional connection, such as date nights, shared hobbies and sharing meals together.

- Continuously learn and grow together, supporting each other's personal development and growth.

4.6 Expressing Love and Affection:

Expressions of love and affection contribute to emotional intimacy.

Practice these **KEYS**:

- Verbalize your love and affection through sincere compliments, "I love you" messages, or love letters.

- Show physical affection through hugs, kisses, holding hands and cuddling.

- Engage in small acts of kindness and thoughtfulness to demonstrate your love and care.

- Celebrate your spouse's qualities, achievements and milestones.

Nurturing emotional intimacy is an ongoing process that requires patience, openness, understanding, vulnerability and commitment to deepening your connection and intentional effort. By creating a safe space, sharing feelings and experiences, cultivating empathy, providing emotional support, dedicating quality time, expressing love and affection, and fostering trust and forgiveness, you can deepen the emotional bond in your marriage. Remember, emotional intimacy evolves and grows over time. As you nurture emotional intimacy, you will create a foundation of love, trust, and understanding that will sustain and enrich your marriage for years to come.

Chapter 5
Building Trust

"Trust is the fragile thread that weaves hearts together."

Trust is the cornerstone of a strong and resilient marriage. It is the anchor that keeps the marriage steady. It forms the foundation upon which love, intimacy, vulnerability and growth can flourish. In this chapter, we will explore the importance of trust in a marriage and discuss practical ways to build, maintain, and restore trust in your relationship.

5.1 Recognizing the Importance of Trust

Trust forms the foundation of a healthy and fulfilling marriage. It enables you and your spouse to feel secure, respected, and emotionally connected.

Practice these **KEYS**:

- Trust is earned over time through consistent actions and behaviors that demonstrate reliability and honesty.

- Trust encourages open communication, vulnerability, and the sharing of thoughts, feelings, and concerns.

- Cultivating trust enhances intimacy, deepens emotional connection, and promotes overall relationship satisfaction.

5.2 Open and Honest Communication:

Open and honest communication is crucial for cultivating trust.

Practice these **KEYS**:

- Create a safe and non-judgmental space where you and your spouse can feel comfortable expressing their thoughts, feelings, and concerns freely.

- Be transparent and truthful in your conversations, even when discussing difficult topics.

- Practice active listening and demonstrate empathy by seeking to understand your spouse's perspective.

- Foster a culture of open dialogue, encouraging the sharing of thoughts, feelings, and concerns.

5.3 Consistency and Reliability:

Consistency and reliability are key factors in cultivating trust.

Practice these **KEYS**:

- Keep your promises and honor your commitments to demonstrate your dependability.

- Be reliable and follow through on your words and actions consistently.

- Avoid making commitments you cannot fulfill and communicate any changes or delays promptly.

- Show up for your spouse consistently and be present in their life.

5.4 Demonstrating Trustworthiness:

Actions speak louder than words when it comes to demonstrating trustworthiness.

Practice these **KEYS**:
- Be accountable for your actions and take responsibility for your mistakes.

- Be transparent about your intentions, plans, and actions.

- Avoid deception, lies, or hiding important information.

- Demonstrate integrity by aligning your words and actions.

5.5 Trust-Building Activities:

Engaging in trust-building activities can strengthen the foundation of trust in your marriage.

Practice these **KEYS**:
- Collaborate on shared projects or goals, fostering a sense of unity and teamwork.

- Establish and maintain healthy boundaries that respect each other's individuality and needs.

- Engage in activities that require trust, such as team-building exercises or adventure sports.

- Prioritize quality time together to deepen emotional connection and understanding.

5.6 Trust, Repair and Rebuilding:

Sometimes trust may be broken or damaged.

Practice these **KEYS**:
- Acknowledge the breach of trust and express genuine remorse.
- Engage in open and honest communication about the impact of the betrayal and the steps needed for rebuilding trust.
- Demonstrate consistent and trustworthy behavior over time.
- Seek professional help, if necessary, to navigate the healing process.

5.7 Forgiveness and Healing:

In any relationship, mistakes and conflicts are inevitable. The ability to forgive and heal is crucial for cultivating trust.

Practice these **KEYS**:
- Practice forgiveness as a means of letting go past hurts and fostering healing.
- Communicate openly about the impact of any breaches of trust and work together on rebuilding trust.
- Seek professional help, such as couples therapy, if needed, to navigate trust-related challenges.

- Be patient with the healing process and commit to rebuilding trust over time.

5.8 Trust, Patience and Forgiveness:

Building and maintaining trust is essential for emotional intimacy.

Practice these **KEYS**:

- Honor your commitments and be reliable, building a foundation of trust.

- Be honest and transparent, even when it's difficult.

- Practice forgiveness and let go of past hurts to foster emotional healing and growth.

- Communicate openly about your needs and expectations and work together to rebuild and strengthen trust.

Trust is a fundamental pillar of a healthy and thriving marriage. By fostering open communication, demonstrating consistency and reliability, practicing trustworthiness, engaging in trust building activities, and navigating trust repair and forgiveness, you can build and maintain a strong foundation of trust in your relationship. Remember, trust is an ongoing commitment that requires continuous effort and nurturing, but the rewards of a trusting marriage are immeasurable.

Chapter 6
Ownership & Accountability

"Don't add an excuse to your apology."

Taking ownership and accountability for your actions and choices are crucial aspects of building a healthy and thriving marriage. It involves recognizing and accepting responsibility for the impact of your behavior on your relationship. In this chapter, we will explore the importance of personal accountability in a marriage and discuss practical ways to embrace ownership and foster growth and harmony in your marriage.

6.1 Personal Accountability:

Personal accountability is the willingness to accept responsibility for your actions, decisions, and consequences. It means being honest with yourself and recognizing the effect your choices are having on your relationship.

Practice these **KEYS**:

- Personal accountability fosters trust, respect, and mutual understanding in your marriage.

- It allows for open and honest communication, as you and your spouse take a closer look at what you're adding to or taking away from the relationship.

- Embracing personal accountability promotes personal growth, self-awareness, and the opportunity to make positive changes.

- Embrace a mindset of personal growth and continuous improvement.

- Take responsibility for your part in conflicts, acknowledging any role you played in the issue.

6.2 Self-Reflection and Awareness:

Self-reflection and self-awareness are essential for taking ownership and accountability.

Practice these **KEYS**:

- Acknowledge and accept the impact of your actions on your spouse and the relationship.

- Apologize sincerely and take ownership of any harm caused, demonstrating genuine remorse.

- Avoid blaming others or making excuses, as this hinders personal growth and undermines trust.

- Be accountable for your mistakes and commit to learning from them to avoid repetition.

6.3 Accept Responsibility:

Accepting responsibility is a courageous step towards personal growth and relationship improvement.

Practice these **KEYS**:

- Acknowledge and accept the impact of your actions on your spouse and the relationship.

- Apologize sincerely and take ownership of any harm caused, demonstrating genuine remorse.

- Avoid blaming others or making excuses, as this hinders personal growth and undermines trust.

- Be accountable for your mistakes and commit to learning from them to avoid repetition.

6.4 Open Communication:

Open communication plays a key role in taking ownership and accountability.

Practice these **KEYS**:

- Foster an environment of open and honest communication with your spouse.

- Be receptive to feedback and constructive criticism without becoming defensive.

- Express your thoughts and feelings authentically, while also actively listening to your spouse's perspective.

- Take responsibility for any communication breakdowns and work on improving your communication skills.

6.5 Acknowledge Mistakes and Apologize:

Acknowledging mistakes and offering sincere apologies is crucial for taking ownership and accountability.

Practice these **KEYS**:

- Be honest with yourself and admit when you have made a mistake or hurt your spouse.

- Offer a genuine and heartfelt apology, taking responsibility for your actions.

- Avoid making excuses or shifting blame onto others.

- Make amends and demonstrate through your actions that you are committed to positive change.

6.6 Making Amends and Restoring Trust:

When trust is damaged, making amends is vital for rebuilding the foundation of your marriage.

Practice these **KEYS**:

- Take active steps to repair the harm caused by your actions and rebuild trust.

- Communicate openly with your spouse about their feelings and needs in the healing process.

- Show consistency in your behavior and take actions that demonstrate trustworthiness over time.

6.7 Commitment to Growth and Change:

Taking ownership and accountability requires a commitment to personal growth and positive change.

Practice these **KEYS**:

- Reflect on areas where you can improve as an individual and as a spouse.

- Set realistic goals for personal development and actively work towards them.

- Invest in acquiring new skills, knowledge, and behaviors that contribute positively to your relationship.

- Embrace a growth mindset, viewing challenges and mistakes as opportunities for learning and development.

6.8 Sustaining Accountability:

Sustaining accountability requires consistent effort and commitment.

Practice these **KEYS**:
- Regularly assess your actions and choices to ensure alignment with your values and commitments.

- Hold yourself accountable for the promises you make to your spouse.

6.9 Support and Encouragement:

Supporting and encouraging your spouse in their journey of personal accountability is essential for a thriving marriage.

Practice these **KEYS**:
- Offer support and encouragement as your spouse takes ownership and accountability for their actions.

- Create a safe and non-judgmental space where you and your spouse can grow and learn from each other's mistakes.

- Engage in ongoing self-reflection and seek feedback from your spouse to monitor your progress.

- Cultivate a support system of friends or family who can hold you accountable.

Taking ownership and accountability for your actions and choices is a transformative practice that can positively impact your marriage. By cultivating self-reflection and awareness, fostering open communication, acknowledging mistakes, committing to growth and change, learning from conflicts, and sustaining accountability, you can foster personal responsibility and contribute to a healthy and thriving marriage. Remember, your individual growth and accountability are essential.

Chapter 7
Prioritizing Quality Time

"Spending time together should be fun, not forced."

In the hustle and bustle of daily life, it's easy for couples to neglect the importance of spending quality time together. However, prioritizing dedicated time for your marriage is crucial for building and maintaining a strong and connected relationship. In this chapter, we will explore the significance of prioritizing quality time in your marriage and discuss practical strategies to make it a priority in your busy lives.

7.1 Quality Time:

Quality time is the intentional and focused attention you give to your spouse. It allows you to nurture your relationship, deepen your understanding of each other, and create lasting memories.

Practice these **KEYS**:

- Quality time promotes emotional connection and intimacy.

- It helps strengthen the foundation of trust and support in your marriage.

- Regular quality time enhances communication, reduces stress and builds resilience.

7.2 The Importance of Quality Time:

Quality time is more than just being physically present with your spouse. It involves intentional engagement, active listening, and creating meaningful experiences together.

Practice these **KEYS**:

- Regular quality time helps to rejuvenate your marriage and enhance overall relationship satisfaction.

- It provides an opportunity to communicate, share thoughts, dreams, and concerns.

7.3 Making Time for Each Other:

Carving out dedicated time for your spouse is crucial.

Practice these **KEYS**:

- Assess your schedules and find pockets of time that can be reserved exclusively for your relationship.

- Prioritize your spouse by making them a top commitment in your schedule.

- Set aside dedicated time for meaningful connection, free from distractions.

- Engage in shared activities or hobbies that foster emotional closeness and create lasting memories.

- Plan regular date nights or weekend getaways to reconnect and deepen your emotional bond.

7.4 Assess Your Time Commitments:

Take a close look at your current time commitments and identify areas where you can make room for quality time.

Practice these **KEYS**:

Evaluate your daily and weekly routines to identify time available for quality interactions.

- Determine if there are any activities or commitments that can be adjusted or eliminated to make room for quality time.

- Discuss with your spouse the importance of prioritizing quality time and explore potential scheduling options.

7.5 Creating Routines and Traditions:

Establishing routines and traditions can provide structure and ensure regular quality time in your marriage.

Practice these **KEYS**:

- Celebrate holidays and special occasions in ways that reflect your shared values and create lasting memories.

- Create traditions unique to your relationship, such as annual getaways or personal routines that signify love and commitment.

- Honor and maintain existing family or cultural traditions that are important to either of you.

- Develop shared rituals, such as cooking together, taking walks and exercising together.

- Create routines around meals, such as cooking together or having a weekly date night.

7.6 Unplugging from Technology:

In today's digital age, it's essential to unplug from technology to fully engage in quality time.

Practice these **KEYS**:

- Designate tech-free zones or time periods when you both agree to put away devices and focus solely on each other.

- Put away smartphones, turn off notifications, and resist the temptation to check social media or emails.

- Prioritize genuine face-to-face interaction and be fully present in the moment.

- Set boundaries on phone or screen usage during quality time together.

- Engage in activities that encourage active engagement and interaction without distractions.

7.7 Date Nights and Special Occasions:

Date nights and special occasions provide opportunities for focused and romantic time together.

Practice these **KEYS**:

- Plan regular date nights, whether it's a dinner out, a movie night at home, or a shared hobby or interest.

- Surprise your spouse with thoughtful gestures and small surprises to make ordinary days feel extraordinary.

- Explore new activities or revisit favorite places that hold significance for both of you.

7.8 Exploring Shared Interests:

Engaging in shared interests and hobbies can strengthen your connection and provide opportunities for quality time.

Practice these **KEYS**:

- Discover shared interests or hobbies and plan activities around them.

- Take turns choosing activities or alternate between each other's interests.

- Be open to trying new experiences together, as it can foster excitement and deepen your connection.

- Participate in activities that allow for collaboration, teamwork, and shared accomplishments.

7.9 Make the Most of Everyday Moments:

Quality time doesn't always have to be elaborate, planned or require grand gestures. Take advantage of everyday moments.

Practice these **KEYS**:

- Find joy and connection in simple activities like cooking together, taking walks, watching the sunset or cuddling up to watch a movie.

- Use daily routines, such as mealtime or bedtime to connect and engage with one another.

- Practice gratitude and express appreciation for the small moments of quality time that occur naturally throughout the day.

- Find joy in simple activities like taking a walk, watching a sunset, or cuddling up to watch a movie.

- Engage in small acts of kindness and gestures that show your love and appreciation.

Prioritizing quality time in your marriage is an investment in your relationship's long-term health and happiness. By making time for each other, unplugging from technology, enjoying date nights, engaging in quality conversations, exploring shared hobbies, and creating rituals and traditions, you can deepen your emotional connection and create a lifetime of cherished memories. Remember, investing time and effort into quality moments with your spouse is a priceless gift that will enrich your marriage for years to come.

Chapter 8
Cultivating Respect

"Harsh words and negative actions rub the heart like sandpaper ."

Respect is a fundamental pillar of a healthy and fulfilling relationship. It forms the foundation for trust, communication, and emotional safety between you and your spouse. In this chapter, we will explore the importance of cultivating respect in your relationship and discuss practical strategies to foster a culture of respect and honor within your marriage.

8.1 The Significance of Respect:

Respect is the fundamental building block of a strong and loving relationship.

Practice these **KEYS**:

- Respect gives you and your spouse the ability to feel valued, heard, and validated.

- It creates an environment where you and your spouse can express themselves freely and without fear of judgment.

- Cultivating respect gives a sense of equality, dignity, and appreciation for each other's worth.

8.2 Active Listening and Valuing Perspectives:

Respectful communication involves active listening and valuing each other's perspectives.

Practice these **KEYS**:

- Practice attentive and non-judgmental listening, giving your full attention to your spouse.

- Validate your spouse's thoughts, feelings, and opinions, even if you disagree.

- Avoid interrupting or dismissing your spouse's ideas, allowing them to fully express themselves.

- Engage in constructive dialogue and find common ground through mutual understanding.

8.3 Honoring Boundaries:

Respecting each other's boundaries is crucial for a healthy relationship.

Practice these **KEYS**:

- Communicate openly about personal boundaries and establish clear expectations.

- Respect each other's decisions and avoid pressuring or coercing your spouse into anything they are not comfortable with.

- Seek consent and avoid making assumptions about your spouse's wants, needs or desires.

- Respect their unique viewpoint.

8.4 Kindness and Constructive Communication:

Respectful communication involves speaking with kindness and choosing words carefully.

Practice these **KEYS**:

- Use "I" statements to express your thoughts and feelings without attacking or blaming your spouse.

- Avoid derogatory language, insults, or name calling, as these undermine respect.

- Practice constructive communication by focusing on solutions rather than dwelling on problems.

- Use words that are considerate, gentle and non-blaming.

- Express your concerns or disagreements in a calm and compassionate manner.

8.5 Differences and Individuality:

Respect involves embracing and appreciating the unique qualities and differences between you and your spouse.

Practice these **KEYS**:

- Celebrate and value each other's strengths, talents, and perspectives.

- Recognize that differences in opinion or interests can enrich your marriage.

- Avoid trying to change or control your spouse to fit your expectations; instead, embrace their individuality.

8.6 Resolving Conflicts Respectfully:

Conflict is a natural part of any relationship, but it can be handled with respect and compassion.

Practice these **KEYS**:

- Approach conflicts as a team. Work together towards a resolution, rather than a battle to be won.

- Listen attentively and express your thoughts and feelings respectfully.

- Listen actively to your spouse's concerns and validate their feelings.

- Avoid personal attacks or belittling your spouse during disagreements.

- Stay on topic and focus on the issue at hand.

- Seek compromise and find mutually beneficial solutions.

8.7 Modeling Respectful Behavior:

Modeling respectful behavior sets a positive example for your marriage.

Practice these **KEYS**:

- Treat your spouse with kindness, courtesy and consideration.

- Show appreciation for your spouse's efforts, contributions and strengths.

- Avoid speaking negatively about your spouse to others.

- Demonstrate respect, not only in private but also in public and social settings.

Cultivating respect is essential for nurturing a strong and harmonious marriage. By honoring boundaries, practicing active listening and empathy, speaking with kindness, appreciating differences, resolving conflicts respectfully and modeling respectful behavior creates a culture of respect that strengthens the foundation of your marriage. Remember, respect is a two-way street that requires ongoing effort and commitment by you and your spouse.

Chapter 9
Resolving Conflicts Peacefully

"Anger is temporary, but its damage can be permanent."

onflict is a natural and inevitable part of any relationship. However, how you navigate and resolve conflict can significantly impact the health and longevity of your marriage. In this chapter, we will explore the importance of resolving conflict constructively and provide practical strategies to navigate disagreements in a healthy and productive manner.

9.1 Understanding Conflict in Marriage:

Conflict arises from differences in opinions, needs and expectations. It can be an opportunity for growth and strengthening your marriage if handled constructively.

Practice these **KEYS**:

- Conflict is normal and inevitable, but it doesn't have to be destructive.

- Unresolved conflict can lead to resentment, distance and damage the foundation of your marriage.

- Constructive conflict resolution promotes understanding, compromise, and deeper connection.

- Conflict provides an opportunity to address underlying issues and improve the marriage.

- It allows for the expression of differing viewpoints, needs, and desires.

9.2 Cultivating a Positive Mindset:

A positive mindset is essential when approaching conflict.

Practice these **KEYS**:

- View conflict as an opportunity for growth, understanding, and finding mutually beneficial solutions.

- Embrace a mindset of collaboration rather than competition.

- Focus on the issue at hand, rather than attacking your spouse personally.

9.3 Creating a Safe and Supportive Environment:

A safe and supportive environment is essential for resolving conflict constructively.

Practice these **KEYS**:

- Establish ground rules for communication, such as no name-calling or interrupting.

- Ensure you and your spouse feel heard and validated during discussions.

- Create an atmosphere of trust, where vulnerabil-ity and honesty are encouraged.

- Take breaks if emotions escalate to allow for self-reflection and calming down.

9.4 Practicing Active Problem-Solving:

Active problem-solving is key to resolving conflict constructively.

Practice these **KEYS**:
- Define the issue at hand and clarify each person's perspective.

- Brainstorm potential solutions together, considering the needs and desires of you and your spouse.

- Evaluate the pros and cons of each solution and seek a compromise that satisfies both parties.

- Implement the chosen solution and assess its effectiveness over time.

9.5 Finding Common Ground:

Finding common ground is crucial for resolving conflict and reaching mutually satisfactory solutions.

Practice these **KEYS**:
- Identify and focus on shared goals or values that you both can agree upon.

- Seek areas of compromise and explore alternative solutions.

- Collaborate to find win-win outcomes that meet you and your spouse's needs.

- Remember that resolving conflict is not about winning or losing but about finding a resolution that honors both perspectives.

9.6 Managing Emotions:

Managing emotions is crucial when resolving conflict constructively.

Practice these **KEYS**:

- Take responsibility for your own emotions and avoid blaming your spouse for how you feel.

- Practice emotional regulation techniques, such as deep breathing or taking a short break to calm down.

- Use "I" statements to express your emotions and needs without attacking or criticizing your spouse.

9.7 Taking a Break:

In heated or escalated conflicts, it may be necessary to take a break to cool down and regain perspective.

Practice these **KEYS**:

- Agree on a mutually agreed-upon signal or code word to indicate when a break is needed.

- Step away from the conflict temporarily, engaging in self-soothing activities such as deep breathing or taking a walk.

- Return to the discussion when you and your spouse are calmer and more open to productive dialogue.

9.8 Learning and Growing from Conflict:

Conflict can be an opportunity for personal growth and learning.

Practice these **KEYS**:

- Reflect on the underlying causes or patterns that contribute to conflict.

- Identify areas for personal improvement and commit to making positive changes.

- Use conflict as a chance to deepen your understanding of each other and strengthen your connection.

9.9 Conflict Resolution:

Conflict is a natural part of any relationship, and effective communication is essential for resolving conflict in a healthy and constructive manner.

Practice these **KEYS**:

- Approach conflict as an opportunity for growth and understanding, rather than a competition.

- Listen attentively to your spouse's viewpoint, seeking to understand their concerns and emotions.

- Express your thoughts, feelings and needs without attacking or criticizing.

- Look for common ground and strive for compromise.

- Focus on finding solutions rather than winning the argument.

- Take breaks if emotions escalate, and reconvene when both of you are calmer.

- Practice forgiveness and let go of past grievances to move forward.

Resolving conflict constructively is an essential skill for a healthy and thriving marriage. By cultivating a positive mindset, creating a safe environment, practicing active problem-solving, managing emotions, and embracing conflict as an opportunity for growth, you can navigate conflict with grace and strengthen your bond. Remember, conflict is natural, but how you handle it can shape the course of your marriage.

Chapter 10
Maintaining Physical Intimacy

"Physical Intimacy can create a sense of connection and closeness that strengthens the bond."

P hysical intimacy plays a vital role in a healthy and fulfilling marriage. It encompasses more than just sexual activity; it involves closeness, affection, and a deep emotional connection. In this chapter, we will explore the importance of maintaining physical intimacy in your marriage and provide practical strategies for nurturing this essential aspect of your relationship.

10.1 Understanding Physical Intimacy:

Physical intimacy strengthens the bond and includes a range of expressions, from holding hands and hugging to sexual intimacy.

Practice these **KEYS**:

- Physical intimacy strengthens the emotional bond between you and your spouse.

- It promotes feelings of love, security and overall relationship satisfaction.

- Regular physical intimacy contributes to a sense of connection, passion, and well-being.

10.2 Communicating Needs and Desires:

Effective communication is vital for maintaining physical intimacy.

Practice these **KEYS**:

- Discuss your needs, desires and boundaries openly and honestly.

- Listen attentively to your spouse's preferences and concerns without judgment.

- Regularly check in with each other to ensure you both feel heard and understood.

- Be receptive to feedback and willing to explore new experiences together.

- Share your fantasies, preferences and concerns in a non-judgmental and compassionate manner.

10.3 Prioritizing Quality Time for Intimacy:

Creating dedicated time for physical intimacy is crucial for maintaining a satisfying sexual connection.

Practice these **KEYS**:

- Set aside specific times for intimacy in your schedule.

- Create a comfortable and inviting environment that encourages relaxation and intimacy.

- Focus on quality over quantity, making the most of the time you have together.

- Experiment with different activities and techniques to keep the spark alive.

10.4 Taking Care of Physical Health:

Physical well-being is closely linked to sexual health and intimacy.

Practice these **KEYS**:

- Maintain a healthy lifestyle through regular exercise, proper nutrition and adequate rest.

- Address any physical health concerns or conditions that may affect your sexual relationship.

- Remember that physical intimacy extends beyond sexual activity and can involve non-sexual touch, massages, or simply being present with each other.

10.5 Adapting to Life Changes:

Life changes and transitions can impact physical intimacy. Adaptation and flexibility are key.

Practice these **KEYS**:

- Communicate openly about how life changes, such as parenthood or career shifts, may affect your physical relationship.

- Be patient and understanding with each other during times of transition.

- Seek creative solutions to maintain intimacy, such as scheduling date nights or exploring new ways to connect physically.

- Embrace the ebb and flow of physical intimacy in your marriage, understanding that it may fluctuate over time.

Maintaining physical intimacy is vital for a thriving and fulfilling marriage. By communicating about needs and desires, prioritizing quality time, nurturing emotional connection, taking care of physical health, and adapting to life changes, you can establish a strong and satisfying physical relationship with your spouse. Remember, physical intimacy is an evolving aspect of your marriage that requires ongoing attention, effort and open communication.

Chapter 11
Keeping the Romance Alive

"Don't ever stop dating your wife, don't ever stop flirting with your husband."

Romance is a vital element that adds spark, passion, and connection to your marriage. It keeps the flame of love burning brightly and deepens your emotional bond as a couple. In this chapter, we will explore strategies and ideas for keeping the romance alive in your marriage, igniting passion, and creating a loving and vibrant relationship.

11.1 Prioritizing Quality Time Together:

Quality time is the foundation of a romantic relationship. It allows you to connect on a deeper level and create lasting memories.

Practice these **KEYS**:

- Schedule regular date nights or romantic outings to spend dedicated time together.

- Disconnect from distractions like phones or work and focus solely on each other.

- Engage in activities that you both enjoy and that promote bonding and intimacy.

- Express affection, both verbally and physically, to nurture a sense of closeness.

11.2 Express Love and Affection:

Continuously express love and affection to keep the romance alive. Small gestures and acts of affection can have a significant impact on your connection.

Practice these **KEYS**:

- Engage in physical touch, such as holding hands, hugging, or cuddling.

- Surprise your spouse with kisses, love notes, or affectionate text messages.

- Compliment and appreciate each other's physical appearance and inner qualities.

- Show gratitude for your spouse's presence in your life.

11.3 Thoughtful Gestures and Surprises:

Small, thoughtful gestures and surprises can go a long way in keeping the romance fresh, exciting and alive. Surprise your spouse with acts of love and kindness.

Practice these **KEYS**:

- Write love notes or leave little surprises for your spouse to find.

- Plan unexpected romantic getaways or weekend retreats.

- Prepare their favorite meal or treat them to a special date at home.

- Offer spontaneous acts of affection, such as hugs, kisses, or gentle touches.

11.4 Open Communicate About Desires and Fantasies:

Keeping the romance alive involves open and honest communication about your desires and fantasies. Create a safe space where you can share your deepest desires and explore new experiences together.

Practice these **KEYS**:

- Initiate conversations about your sexual desires and preferences.

- Share your fantasies and listen to your spouse's without judgment.

- Explore new ways to add excitement and variety to your intimate life.

- Be open to trying new things and mutually satisfying each other's desires.

11.5 Nurture Emotional Intimacy:

Emotional intimacy is a vital component of a romantic relationship. Cultivate a deep emotional connection with your spouse to strengthen the romance.

Practice these **KEYS**:

- Practice open and honest communication, sharing your thoughts, fears, and dreams.

- Listen attentively and offer emotional support during both joyful and challenging times.

- Show empathy and understanding toward your spouse's emotions.

- Engage in activities that promote emotional connection, such as deep conversations or sharing favorite memories.

11.6 Physical Intimacy and Affection:

Physical intimacy is a crucial aspect of keeping the romance alive in your marriage. It deepens your emotional connection and strengthens the bond between you and your spouse.

Practice these **KEYS**:

- Maintain regular physical affection, such as hugging, kissing, and cuddling.

- Engage in intimate moments of closeness, even without the expectation of sex.

- Prioritize intimacy by setting aside time for physical connection and pleasure.

- Be attentive to your spouse's needs and desires, and communicate your own openly.

11.7 Maintain Intimacy in the Bedroom:

Physical intimacy is a significant aspect of a romantic relationship. Prioritize maintaining a healthy and satisfying intimate life with your spouse.

Practice these **KEYS**:

- Communicate openly about your desires, fantasies, and boundaries.

- Explore new ways to enhance intimacy and pleasure together.

- Prioritize intimacy and create a conducive environment for physical connection.

Keeping the romance alive requires continuous effort and attention. By prioritizing quality time, expressing love and affection, embracing surprises, nurturing emotional intimacy and maintaining intimacy in the bedroom, you can create a romantic and passionate marriage. Remember that romance is unique to each couple, so adapt these suggestions to fit your own dynamic and discover what works best for you and your spouse.

Chapter 12
Practicing Forgiveness

"Be intentional about letting go of resentment and anger."

Forgiveness is a powerful tool for healing and maintaining a healthy marriage. Inevitably, mistakes, conflicts, and misunderstandings will occur in any relationship. Learning to practice forgiveness can help you move past these challenges and cultivate a more resilient and loving bond. In this chapter, we will explore the importance of forgiveness in your marriage and provide practical strategies for embracing forgiveness.

12.1 The Power of Forgiveness:

Forgiveness is not about condoning or forgetting the hurtful actions or words of your spouse. It is about releasing the negative emotions and allowing space for healing and growth.

Practice these **KEYS**:

- Forgiveness frees you from carrying the burden of resentment, anger and bitterness.

- It allows for the possibility of repairing and rebuilding trust in your marriage.

- Practicing forgiveness nurtures compassion, empathy and a deeper understanding of your spouse.

12.2 Cultivating a Forgiving Mindset:

Developing a forgiving mindset is essential for practicing forgiveness.

Practice these **KEYS**:
- Recognize that forgiveness is a gift you give yourself, allowing you to move forward and let go of negative emotions.

- Challenge negative thought patterns and replace them with compassionate and understanding perspectives.

- Practice self-compassion, acknowledging your own mistakes and imperfections.

- Focus on the positive aspects of your spouse and your marriage rather than dwelling on past hurts.

12.3 The Nature of Mistakes:

Recognize that making mistakes is a part of being human. Both you and your spouse will inevitably fall short at times.

Practice these **KEYS**:
- Acknowledge that everyone is prone to errors, and no one is perfect.

- Understand that mistakes can be opportunities for growth and learning.

- Cultivate a mindset that views mistakes as opportunities for forgiveness and understanding.

12.4 Practicing Self-Compassion:

Forgiveness begins with extending compassion and forgiveness to yourself.

Practice these **KEYS**:

- Recognize that holding onto anger and resentment towards your spouse can harm your emotional well-being.

- Understand that you have the power to choose forgiveness as an act of self-love and personal growth.

- Be gentle with yourself, acknowledging that healing takes time and that it is okay to set boundaries and prioritize your emotional needs.

12.5 Healing and Rebuilding Trust:

Forgiveness paves the way for healing and rebuilding trust in your marriage.

Practice these **KEYS**:

- Be patient and understanding, recognizing that rebuilding trust takes time.

- Follow through on your promises and commitments, demonstrating consistency and reliability.

- Engage in open and transparent communication, fostering an environment of honesty and vulnerability.

12.6 Letting Go and Moving Forward:

The final step in practicing forgiveness is letting go of the past and embracing a future free from resentment.

Practice these **KEYS**:

- Release the need for revenge or punishment, understanding that holding onto anger only harms you.

- Focus on personal growth and learning from past experiences.

- Practice self-care and engage in activities that promote your well-being.

- Embrace a mindset of gratitude and appreciation for the positive aspects of your relationship.

Practicing forgiveness is a transformative and essential element of a healthy and thriving relationship. By understanding the power of forgiveness, reflecting on your emotions, practicing self-compassion, engaging in open communication, re-building trust, and letting go of the past, you can cultivate a relationship rooted in understanding, healing, and growth. Remember, forgiveness is a choice and a process that requires effort, compassion, and a commitment to the well-being of your marriage.

Chapter 13
Compromise

"It can't be your way every time."

Compromise is an essential skill for maintaining a healthy and balanced marriage. It involves finding common ground, negotiating differences, and making joint decisions that consider both you and your spouse's needs and desires. In this chapter, we will explore the importance of compromise and discuss practical strategies for fostering compromise and cooperation within your relationship.

13.1 Understanding the Value of Compromise:

Compromise is not about one person winning and the other losing; it is about finding a middle ground that honors both you and your spouse's needs and desires. Recognize the value of compromise in creating a harmonious and balanced relationship.

Practice these **KEYS**:

- Understand that compromise is not a sign of weakness but a strength that promotes understanding and growth.

- Appreciate that compromise allows you and your spouse to feel heard, respected, and valued.

- Recognize that compromise fosters a cooperative and collaborative approach to problem-solving.

- Understand that compromise does not mean one partner always gets their way or that decisions are always divided equally.

13.2 Effective Communication and Active Listening:

Effective communication and active listening are essential for successful compromise. Engage in open and honest dialogue to understand each other's perspectives, needs, and concerns.

Practice these **KEYS**:

- Express your thoughts and feelings clearly and respectfully.

- Listen attentively to your spouse's point of view without interrupting or becoming defensive.

- Ask questions to gain a deeper understanding of their perspective.

- Seek common ground and areas of agreement as a foundation for compromise.

13.3 Open and Respectful Communication:

Effective communication sets the stage for successful compromise. Create an environment where you and your spouse can express their thoughts, needs, and concerns openly and respectfully.

Practice these **KEYS**:

- Practice active listening and seek to understand each other's viewpoints.

- Clearly express your own thoughts and desires without dismissing or belittling your spouse.

- Use "I" statements to express your needs and concerns, focusing on your perspective rather than attacking your spouse.

13.4 Identify and Prioritize Needs:

To reach a compromise, it is crucial to identify and prioritize your own needs and those of your spouse.

Practice these **KEYS**:

- Reflect on your individual needs and desires in the situation at hand.

- Encourage your spouse to share their needs openly and honestly.

- Discuss and clarify the importance and significance of each need.

13.5 Identify Shared Goals and Priorities:

Compromise becomes easier when you both identify shared goals and priorities. By focusing on common objectives, you can work together towards finding solutions that align with you and your spouse's desires.

Practice these **KEYS**:

- Have discussions to identify and prioritize shared goals, such as financial stability, raising children, or career aspirations.

- Align your decisions and compromises with these shared goals and priorities.

- Keep these goals in mind during challenging moments to maintain a sense of purpose and unity.

13.6 Seek Win-Win Solutions:

Aim for win-win solutions where you and your spouse's needs and desires are met to the best extent possible. This approach fosters a sense of fairness and satisfaction for both you and your spouse.

Practice these **KEYS**:

- Brainstorm creative solutions that accommodate both you and your spouse's interests.

- Be open to alternative perspectives and explore different options.

- Look for compromises that maximize benefits for you and your spouse rather than settling for "halfway" solutions.

13.7 Focus on Long-Term Goals and the Big Picture:

When faced with challenges, it is essential to focus on long-term goals and the big picture of your marriage.

Practice these **KEYS**:

- Keep in mind the overarching values and vision you share as a couple.

- Evaluate the significance of the issue in the grand scheme of your relationship.

- Consider the impact of your actions on the overall well-being and happiness of you and your spouse.

13.8 Patience and Understanding:

Compromise takes time, patience and understanding. It may require multiple discussions before reaching a satisfactory resolution.

Practice these **KEYS**:
- Be patient with the process and allow space for thoughtful consideration.

- Be understanding of your spouse's perspective and the emotions involved.

- Practice empathy and put yourself in your partner's shoes to gain a deeper understanding of their viewpoint.

- Be willing to make adjustments and revisit the compromise if necessary.

Compromise is an essential skill in building a strong and harmonious marriage. By valuing compromise, practicing effective communication and active listening, identifying and prioritizing needs, engaging in creative problem-solving, embracing win-win solutions, focusing on long-term goals, and practicing patience and understanding, you can foster a spirit of compromise in your relationship that promotes mutual growth, satisfaction, and fulfillment. Remember, compromise is a joint effort that requires you and your spouse to contribute and work together for the benefit of the relationship.

Chapter 14

The Importance of Dating (Systematic and Spontaneous)

"Date like you did before the wedding."

D ating is not just a luxury or a frivolous indulgence; it is an essential component of a healthy and thriving marriage. It provides an opportunity to stay connected, reconnect, have fun together, and prioritize your relationship amidst the busyness of life. In this chapter, we will explore the significance of dating and how it can strengthen your bond, enhance communication, and revitalize your relationship. We will offer practical strategies for making it a regular part of your married life.

14.1 Reconnecting as a Couple:

Dating provides an opportunity to reconnect as a couple outside of the demands and responsibilities of everyday life.

Practice these **KEYS:**

- Set aside dedicated time to focus solely on each other and your relationship.

- Use dating as a chance to deepen your emotional connection and intimacy.

- Engage in activities that bring joy, laughter, and shared experiences.

- Rediscover the reasons why you fell in love and nurture the romantic aspect of your relationship.

14.2 Make Dating a Priority:

To fully benefit from dating, it's crucial to prioritize and commit to making dating a regular part of your marriage.

Practice these **KEYS**:

- Schedule dates in advance and treat them as non-negotiable commitments.

- Block off time on your calendar and communicate with your spouse about the importance of this dedicated time.

- Set realistic expectations and make adjustments when necessary, but strive to maintain consistency in having regular dating times.

14.3 Choosing Activities That Foster Connection:

The activities you choose for date time can greatly impact the level of connection and enjoyment you experience.

Practice these **KEYS**:

- Alternate between planned and spontaneous dates to keep things fresh and exciting.

- Engage in activities that promote meaningful conversation, such as going for a walk, having a picnic, or sharing a meal at a favorite restaurant.

- Explore new experiences together, such as taking a dance class, visiting a museum, or going on an adventure.

- Tailor activities to your shared interests and preferences, ensuring that both you and your spouse feel engaged and enthusiastic.

14.4 Spontaneous Dating:

Dating injects fun, excitement, and variety into your marriage. It breaks the monotony of daily routines and brings a sense of adventure.

Practice these **KEYS**:

- Be creative. Be spontaneous. Date time doesn't always have to be a scheduled day, night, week or month.

- Choose something fun that includes elements you both enjoy, such as dressing up and going out, cooking together or exchanging thoughtful gestures.

14.5 Recharging and Relieving Stress:

Date nights provide a much-needed break from the stressors of daily life. They offer a chance to unwind, relax, and rejuvenate as a couple.

Practice these **KEYS**:

- Take a break from work-related concerns and focus on each other.

- Disconnect from technology to fully engage with your spouse.

- Engage in activities that promote relaxation, such as spa dates or nature walks.

- Create a stress-free environment where you can let go and enjoy each other's company.

14.6 Prioritizing Connection and Communication:

Date nights are an ideal opportunity to enhance your connection and communication as a couple.

Practice these **KEYS**:

- Practice active listening during your date nights, giving each other undivided attention and truly hearing what your spouse has to say.

- Engage in meaningful conversations that go beyond surface-level topics, discussing dreams, aspirations and deeper emotions.

- If the atmosphere allows you can use date time as a space to address any relationship challenges or concerns, approaching them with openness, empathy, and a willingness to find resolutions.

14.7 Adjusting Date Time During Busy Seasons:

Life can get hectic, and there may be times when it's challenging to stick to a regular dating routine. During such busy seasons, adapt and find creative ways to prioritize your connection.

Practice these **KEYS**:

- Plan shorter and more frequent mini-dates, such as a coffee date during a lunch break or a movie night at home after the kids are asleep.

- Look for opportunities to incorporate quality time into your daily routines, such as cooking together, taking evening walks, or having intentional conversations before bedtime.

Dating is not just an indulgence; it is a vital ingredient for a successful and fulfilling marriage. By prioritizing regular date time, you can reconnect as a couple, nurture communication and connection, prioritize emotional intimacy, inject fun and variety, strengthen romance, and relieve stress. Remember, date time is an investment in your relationship and a way to prioritize your love and commitment to each other.

Chapter 15
Meeting Each Other's Needs

"Be Flexible. Working together to meet each other's needs is an essential component of a healthy relationship."

M
eeting each other's needs is an essential aspect of a healthy and fulfilling marriage. It involves understanding and fulfilling the emotional, physical, and relational needs of your partner. In this chapter, we will explore the significance of meeting each other's needs and provide practical strategies for nurturing a mutually satisfying relationship.

15.1 Understanding Individual Needs:

Recognizing and understanding your spouse's needs is the first step towards meeting them effectively. Each person has unique needs that require attention and care. With that uniqueness you will have different emotional, physical, and relational requirements.

Practice these **KEYS**:

- Communicate openly with your spouse about your needs and encourage them to do the same.

- Reflect on your own needs and be aware of any unmet or recurring patterns.

- Listen attentively to your spouse, seeking to understand their perspective and what truly matters to them.

- Be receptive to their feedback and willing to adjust your behaviors and actions accordingly.

15.2 Valuing and Prioritizing Needs:

Once you have a clear understanding of each other's needs, it is essential to value and prioritize them within your relationship. This requires making a conscious effort to ensure that your spouse's needs are not overlooked or neglected.

Practice these **KEYS:**

- Treat your spouse's needs with respect and importance, even if they differ from your own.

- Prioritize meeting their needs alongside your own, creating a mutually supportive and caring dynamic.

- Regularly check in with each other to assess if your needs are being met and make necessary adjustments.

15.3 Supportive Partnership:

Meeting each other's needs involves actively supporting and partnering with your spouse in various aspects of life. It means being a source of strength, encouragement, and assistance.

Practice these **KEYS:**

- Offer practical help and assistance when your spouse is overwhelmed or facing challenges.

- Collaborate on shared responsibilities, such as parenting, household chores, and financial management.

- Be a source of encouragement, celebrating your spouse's achievements and providing reassurance during difficult times.

- Show respect and appreciation for their contributions to the relationship and acknowledge their unique strengths.

15.4 Continual Growth and Learning:

Meeting each other's needs is an ongoing process that requires continual growth and learning as individuals and as a couple. Recognize that needs may change over time, and it is essential to adapt to those changes as a couple.

Practice these **KEYS**:

- Be open to personal growth and self-reflection, recognizing and addressing your own limitations and areas for improvement.

- Embrace flexibility and be willing to adjust your behaviors and actions to accommodate your partner's evolving needs.

- Regularly check in with each other to assess if needs have evolved or if new needs have arisen.

Meeting each other's needs is vital for a strong and fulfilling marriage. By understanding and addressing your spouse's emotional, physical, and relational needs, you can cultivate a loving and supportive partnership. Remember to communicate openly, show empathy, prioritize intimacy and quality time, be flexible and compromising, conduct regular check-ins, and continually grow and learn together. By doing so, you can create a relationship where you both feel understood, cherished, and fulfilled.

Chapter 16
The Importance of Affirmation

"Negative words can sabotage your marriage. Use words that build up your spouse, not tear them down."

Affirmation is a powerful tool that can strengthen the bond between you and your spouse, boost self-esteem, and create a positive atmosphere in your marriage. It involves expressing appreciation, admiration and support for your spouse, creating an atmosphere of love, positivity, and encouragement. In this chapter, we will explore the importance of affirmation in your marriage and provide practical ways to incorporate it into your daily lives.

16.1 Building Emotional Connection:

Affirmation strengthens the emotional connection between you and your spouse. When you express admiration and appreciation for each other, it creates a sense of emotional closeness and deepens your bond.

Practice these **KEYS**:

- Affirmation helps your spouse feel valued, understood, and loved.

- It fosters a positive emotional climate within your marriage, enhancing overall satisfaction.

* Regular affirmation builds a strong foundation of trust and support.

16.2 Boosting Self-Esteem and Confidence:

Affirmation has the power to boost your spouse's self-esteem and confidence. When you acknowledge their strengths, accomplishments, and positive qualities, it reinforces their sense of self-worth.

Practice these **KEYS**:

* Pay attention to your spouse's efforts, achievements, and growth, and express genuine praise and recognition.

* Express genuine compliments and praise for their character, efforts, and achievements.

* Recognize and appreciate their unique qualities, both physical and non-physical.

* Encourage your spouse to pursue their passions and dreams, providing unwavering support and belief in their abilities.

16.3 Nurturing a Positive Atmosphere:

Affirmation contributes to creating a positive and uplifting atmosphere which fosters happiness and resilience in your marriage. When you regularly affirm each other, it becomes easier to navigate challenges and conflicts with love and understanding. It sets the tone for communication, interactions, and overall marital satisfaction.

Practice these **KEYS**:

- Use positive and encouraging language focusing on what you appreciate and love about your spouse.

- Use kind and encouraging words, even during disagreements or difficult conversations.

- Practice gratitude by expressing appreciation for the little things your spouse does.

- Create a habit of affirming each other regularly, whether through words, gestures, texts or writ-ten notes.

16.4 Active Listening and Validation:

Affirmation involves active listening and validation of your spouse's thoughts, feelings, and experiences. It demonstrates empathy and understanding, strengthening your connection.

Practice these **KEYS**:

- Give your full attention when your spouse is speaking, making eye contact and avoid distractions.

- Validate their experiences and emotions by acknowledging and accepting their feelings, even if you don't fully understand or agree.

- Avoid judgment or criticism, creating a safe space for open and honest communication.

16.5 Expressing Love and Appreciation:

Affirmation is a powerful way to express your love and appreciation for your spouse. Verbal and physical displays of affection strengthen the emotional connection and reinforce the love you share.

Practice these **KEYS**:

- Say "I love you" regularly and meaningfully.

- Express specific appreciation for your spouse's actions, kindness, and support.

- Leave thoughtful notes, messages, or surprises that remind your spouse of your love and admiration.

- Show physical affection, such as hugging, holding hands, kissing or offering a gentle touch.

- Express your love through acts of service or thoughtful gestures that show you care.

16.6 Making Affirmation a Daily Habit:

Consistency is key to ensuring that affirmation becomes a natural and integral part of your relationship.

Practice these **KEYS**:

- Make affirmation a daily practice, finding opportunities to express appreciation and love.

- Find small ways throughout the day to uplift your spouse.

- Share highlights from your day and express gratitude for your spouse before going to bed.

Affirmation is a powerful tool that can transform your marriage. By nurturing emotional connection, boosting self-esteem, fostering a positive atmosphere, practicing active listening and validation, expressing love and affection and making affirmation a daily habit, you can create a loving and supportive environment where both you and your spouse feel cherished and valued. Remember, small acts of affirmation can have a big impact on the quality and longevity of your marriage.

Chapter 17
Financial Transparency

"Openly share financial information with your spouse."

F inancial transparency is a crucial aspect of a healthy and successful marriage. It involves open and honest communication about money matters, joint decision-making, and a shared understanding of your financial goals and responsibilities. In this chapter, we will explore why financial transparency is essential in your marriage and provide practical tips for achieving it.

17.1 Building Trust and Unity:

Financial transparency is key to building trust and unity in your marriage. When you and your spouse are open and honest about their financial situation, it creates a sense of transparency and reliability. It establishes a solid foundation for working together towards your shared financial goals.

Practice these **KEYS**:

- Financial Transparency will allow you both to feel included and valued in financial decision-making.

- Financial Transparency eliminates suspicion and fosters trust and understanding.

- Financial transparency minimizes misunderstandings and reduces the potential for conflicts and resentment.

17.2 Sharing Financial Information:

Sharing financial information is essential for transparency in your marriage. It involves openly discussing your income, expenses, debts, assets and financial obligations.

Practice these **KEYS**:

- Set aside dedicated time to review and discuss your finances regularly.

- Share account statements, credit card statements, and any other relevant financial documents with each other.

- Create a joint budget that reflects both of your incomes, expenses, and financial goals.

- Discuss and disclose any outstanding debts or financial commitments.

17.3 Joint Decision-Making:

Financial transparency requires joint decision-making regarding your financial matters. It ensures that both you and your spouse are involved in important financial choices and have a shared understanding of your financial priorities.

Practice these **KEYS**:

- Collaboratively create a plan that reflects your income, expenses, and financial priorities.

- Make major financial decisions together, such as large purchases, investments, or changes in financial strategies.

- Discuss and agree upon financial goals, such as saving for a house, retirement, or educational expenses.

- Seek consensus on budget allocations, expense management, and financial priorities.

- Regularly review your budget together, making adjustments as needed.

- Consult each other before making significant financial commitments.

17.4 Shared Responsibility:

Financial transparency involves shared responsibility for your financial well-being. It requires a collaborative effort in managing your finances and ensuring that both spouses are actively involved.

Practice these **KEYS:**

- Divide financial responsibilities based on each other's strengths and interests.

- Share the task of bill payments, tracking expenses, and maintaining financial records.

- Make joint decisions regarding savings, investments, and financial planning.

- Work together to establish financial habits and practices that support your shared goals.

17.5 Regular Financial Check-Ins:

Regular financial check-ins provide an opportunity to assess progress, address concerns, and make adjustments as needed. They keep you both accountable and ensure that you are on track with your financial goals.

Practice these **KEYS**:

- Schedule regular meetings to review your financial situation together.

- Use these check-ins to discuss any changes in your financial circumstances, income, or expens-es and make adjustments as needed.

- Celebrate milestones and successes in achieving your financial goals together.

Financial transparency is a vital component of a strong and thriving marriage. It builds trust, fosters unity, and promotes open communication about money matters. By sharing financial information, engaging in joint decision-making, conducting regular financial check-ins, taking shared responsibility, seeking professional guidance when needed, and practicing honesty and accountability, you can establish a solid financial foundation that supports your long-term goals and strengthens your relationship. Remember, financial transparency is a journey that requires ongoing effort and communication, but the rewards are well worth it in building a secure and harmonious financial future together.

Chapter 18
Commitment and Faithfulness

"Don't say or do things that make your spouse feel replaceable."

C ommitment and faithfulness are major keys for a strong and lasting marriage. They provide a sense of security, trust, and emotional connection between you and your spouse. In this chapter, we will explore the significance of staying committed and faithful in your marriage and provide practical strategies on how to nurture these essential qualities.

18.1 Building Trust and Security:

Commitment and faithfulness form the foundation of trust and security within a marriage. When both spouse are committed to each other's well-being and remain faithful, it creates an atmosphere of safety and reliability.

Practice these **KEYS**:

- Commitment provides assurance that your spouse is there for you through thick and thin.

- Faithfulness builds trust, knowing that your spouse is devoted to the marriage and values the sacred bond between you.

- Trust and security promotes emotional intimacy and allows the relationship to thrive.

18.2 Honoring Vows and Promises:

Staying committed and faithful means honoring the vows and promises you made to each other on your wedding day. It involves upholding the commitment to love, support, and cherish your spouse in good times and bad.

Practice these **KEYS**:

- Reflect on the vows you exchanged and the promises you made to each other.

- Remind yourself of the importance of keeping those commitments and living up to the promises you made.

- Embrace the responsibility of staying true to your marriage vows, allowing them to guide your actions and decisions.

18.3 Understanding the Impact of Infidelity:

Recognize the devastating impact that infidelity can have on a marriage. Infidelity breaks trust, damages emotional connection, and undermines the foundation of the relationship. Understanding these facts can reinforce the importance of staying committed and faithful.

Practice these **KEYS**:

- Educate yourself about the consequences of infidelity on you, your spouse and the marriage as a whole.

- Acknowledge the emotional pain and trauma caused by infidelity, and commit to protecting your marriage from such harm.

18.4 Resisting Temptation:

Staying committed and faithful requires resisting temptation, both emotionally and physically. It involves making conscious choices to prioritize your marriage and resist actions or situations that could compromise the trust and fidelity within the relationship.

Practice these **KEYS**:

- Stay mindful of potential triggers or situations that may tempt you to stray from your commitment.

- Communicate openly with your spouse about any concerns or challenges you may be facing.

- Establish boundaries and safeguards to protect your marriage from external influences or temptations.

- Seek support from trusted friends, family, or professionals if you are struggling with temptation.

18.5 Nurturing Intimacy and Connection:

Commitment and faithfulness contribute to the nurturing of intimacy and connection within the marriage. They involve prioritizing and investing in the emotional, physical, and sexual aspects of the relationship.

Practice these **KEYS**:

- Cultivate open and honest communication about your emotional and physical needs and desires.

- Create opportunities for quality time and shared experiences that deepen your connection.

- Maintain a healthy and fulfilling sexual relationship, focusing on pleasure, intimacy, and satisfaction for you and your spouse.

- Show affection, appreciation, and love through words and actions on a regular basis.

18.6 Renewing Commitment:

Marriage is a lifelong journey, and staying committed and faithful requires periodic renewal and reaffirmation. It involves actively choosing your spouse and the marriage every day.

Practice these **KEYS**:

- Celebrate anniversaries and milestones as opportunities to reflect on your commitment and the journey you have shared.

- Engage in regular conversations about your shared goals, aspirations, and the future you envision together.

- Continually express love, appreciation, and gratitude for your spouse reminding them of your unwavering dedication.

- Consider renewing your vows or create rituals that symbolize your ongoing commitment to each other.

18.7 Fostering a Supportive and Loving Environment:

Creating a supportive and loving environment in your marriage promotes commitment and faithfulness. When you and your spouse feel valued, respected, and loved, the desire to stay faithful is strengthened.

Practice these **KEYS**:

- Show appreciation for your spouse's contributions to the relationship and express gratitude for their presence in your life.

- Demonstrate love and affection through words, gestures, and physical touch.

- Foster a culture of emotional safety and support, encouraging open and honest communication.

Staying committed and faithful are essential for creating a loving, secure, and fulfilling marriage. By establishing a solid foundation, understanding the impact of infidelity, cultivating trust and communication, nurturing emotional connection, renewing commitment, and fostering a supportive environment, you can strengthen your commitment and deepen your faithfulness to each other. Remember that staying committed and faithful is a daily choice and requires ongoing effort, but the rewards of a strong and enduring marriage are immeasurable.

Chapter 19
Fun And Adventure

*"*Engaging in playful activities can promote a
sense of happiness and reduce tension
and stress*."*

Keeping the element of fun and adventure alive in
your marriage is vital for maintaining a vibrant,
exciting, and fulfilling partnership. In this chapter, we will explore the reasons why having fun and
adventure is important in your marriage and provides
examples of how you can infuse your relationship with
joy and excitement.

19.1 Reigniting the Spark:

Having fun and embarking on adventures together can
reignite the spark in your marriage. Over time, routines
and responsibilities can dampen the excitement and
spontaneity in a relationship. By incorporating fun and
adventurous activities, you reignite the flame and keep
the connection alive.

Practice these **KEYS**:

- Fun and adventure create opportunities to reconnect on a deeper level, rediscovering each
other's interests and passions.

- Shared experiences that bring laughter and joy can help you remember what initially drew you together as a couple.

- Trying new things together fosters a sense of adventure and keeps the relationship fresh and exciting.

Example:

- Plan a surprise date night where you both dress up and go to a new restaurant.

- Participate in an activity neither of you have tried before, such as rock climbing, dancing lessons, a cooking class or a spontaneous road trip to a nearby town you've never visited.

19.2 Strengthening Emotional Bonding:

Engaging in fun activities and adventures strengthens the emotional bond between you and your spouse.

It allows you to create lasting memories and share stories that contribute to a strong sense of connection.

Practice these **KEYS**:
- Enjoying fun experiences together enhances feelings of closeness, intimacy, and friendship.

- Overcoming challenges and stepping outside your comfort zones as a couple builds trust and resilience.

- Laughter and joy release endorphins, which promote positive emotions and create a deeper emotional connection.

Example:

- Plan a weekend getaway to a destination you both have always wanted to visit.

- Explore new sights, indulge in fun activities, and make a conscious effort to fully engage with each other during the trip.

19.3 Building Fond Memories:

Fun and adventurous experiences create a bank of shared memories that strengthen the bond between you and your spouse. These memories serve as a reminder of the joyous moments you've shared, reinforcing your connection and providing a source of happiness during challenging times.

Practice these **KEYS**:

- Creating positive memories helps build a reservoir of love and resilience in your relationship.

- Reflecting on past fun and adventurous experiences strengthens your emotional connection and fosters a sense of nostalgia.

- These memories become a source of comfort and joy, providing a foundation of happiness to draw upon.

Example:

- Plan a yearly tradition, such as a weekend getaway to a new destination, where you can explore new places, try exciting activities, and create unforgettable memories together.

19.4 Reducing Stress and Promoting Well-Being:

Having fun and seeking adventure provides a healthy escape and an outlet for stress relief and promotes over-all well-being in your marriage. Engaging in enjoyable activities together can alleviate tension, enhance your mood, improve emotional and physical health and can help both you and your spouse unwind and recharge.

Practice these **KEYS**:

- Adventure can bring a sense of excitement and anticipation, providing a break from the monotony of routine.

- Laughing together promotes relaxation and can improve physical health by reducing stress hormones.

Example:

- Take up a new hobby or recreational activity together, such as hiking, dancing, or painting. Make it a regular practice to set aside dedicated time for these activities to unwind, have fun and create lasting memories.

Example:

- Plan a regular "game night" where you play board games, card games or video games together. Create a light-hearted and fun atmosphere to let go of stress and enjoy each other's company.

19.5 Enhancing Communication and Teamwork:

Engaging in fun and adventurous activities opens up new avenues for communication and strengthens your overall connection. When you step outside your comfort zone together you develop a deeper understanding of each other and create opportunities for open and lighthearted communication, a spirit of collaboration, problem-solving, and shared decision-making.

Practice these **KEYS**:

- Fun and adventure encourage teamwork and collaboration, strengthening you ability to work together and demonstrate effective communication and problem-solving skills.

- Engaging in new experiences together allows for shared moments of vulnerability, which strengthens trust and intimacy.

- These activities create opportunities for laughter, playfulness, and shared joy, nurturing a positive and vibrant dynamic in your relationship.

Example:

- Take a dance class together, where you can learn new moves, laugh at each other's missteps, and communicate nonverbally through dance. This activity promotes physical closeness, communication, and laughter.

Example:

- Sign up for a cooking class together, where you work as a team to prepare a meal. This not only encourages communication and cooperation but also allows you to explore a new skill and enjoy a delicious outcome.

19.6 Preventing Monotony and Routine:

Fun and adventure serve as a powerful antidote to monotony and routine in your marriage. By intentionally incorporating excitement and novelty, you break free from the mundane and keep your relationship fresh and engaging.

Practice these **KEYS**:

- Engaging in exciting activities and trying new things can reignite a sense of passion and vitality.

- Fun and adventure stimulate creativity, curiosity and a sense of discovery within your relationship.

- Stepping outside your comfort zones together encourages personal growth and expands your shared experiences.

Example:

- Plan a surprise weekend getaway to a destination neither of you has visited before. Explore new sights, try local cuisines, and immerse yourselves in the adventure of discovering a new place together.

Example:

- For our outside enthusiast, plan a weekend camping trip where you can disconnect from technology and immerse yourselves in nature. Engage in outdoor activities such as hiking, stargazing or building a campfire together.

Having fun and seeking adventure in your marriage is not just a luxury; it is an essential ingredient for a thriving and joyful partnership. By incorporating fun and adventurous activities, you can renew the spark, reduce stress, build fond memories, enhance communication and connection, and prevent monotony. Embrace the spirit of adventure, step outside your comfort zone, and create a marriage filled with laughter, excitement, and un-forgettable experiences. Remember, the journey itself becomes the destination, and the memories you create together will enrich your relationship for years to come.

Chapter 20
Avoiding Power Struggles

"Remember, you're on the same team. Always seek Win-Win Solutions."

P ower Struggles in a marriage can create tension, resentment, and strain on the relationship. Maintaining a healthy balance of power and avoiding unnecessary conflicts is crucial for fostering a harmonious and fulfilling marriage. In this chapter, we will explore the reasons why it is not good to have a power struggle in your marriage and provide insights on how to navigate power dynamics in a positive way.

20.1 Erosion of Trust and Power Struggles:

Power struggles undermine the foundation of trust and intimacy in your marriage. When you and your spouse engage in constant battles for control or dominance, it becomes challenging to feel emotionally safe and connected.

Practice these **KEYS**:

- Power struggles can create an atmosphere of competition rather than collaboration.

- Trust is eroded as either spouse may become skeptical of each other's motives and actions.

- They diminish value and contributions, leading to feelings of resentment and dissatisfaction.

- Emotional intimacy suffers, leading to a sense of distance and disconnection.

- Power Struggles can lead to emotional abuse, manipulation and the loss of self-esteem.

- Power Struggles create a cycle of defensiveness and mistrust, hindering the growth of a deep and meaningful bond.

20.2 Communication Breakdown:

Power Struggles often lead to a breakdown in communication between. Instead of open and honest dialogue, conflicts become focused on winning and asserting power. When you or your spouse focus on asserting power rather than listening and understanding each other, meaningful dialogue becomes challenging.

Practice these **KEYS**:

- Power Struggles promote defensiveness and a lack of openness to different perspectives.

- Effective communication becomes difficult when prioritizing being right rather than understanding each other becomes the main focus.

- They can escalate conflicts and prevent the resolution of underlying issues.

- Important issues go unresolved as the focus shifts from problem-solving to maintaining power.

- Emotional and physical needs are left unaddressed, leading to frustration and resentment.

20.3 Neglecting Compromise and Collaboration:

Power Struggles often prevent the practice of compromise and collaboration in a marriage. Instead of working together to find mutually beneficial solutions, either spouse may become entrenched in their own position, further exacerbating the conflict.

Practice these **KEYS**:

- Compromise and collaboration are essential for maintaining a healthy and balanced relationship.

- Power Struggles perpetuate a win-lose mentality, leading to a lack of satisfaction for you and your spouse.

- Neglecting compromise and collaboration limits the growth and development of the relationship, stifling its potential.

20.4 Emotional and Mental Distress:

Engaging in power struggles takes a toll on your personal well-being. The constant conflict, stress and emotional turmoil can lead to significant distress.

Practice these **KEYS**:

- Power Struggles contribute to heightened stress levels and decreased overall happiness, increase levels of anxiety, depression and overall emotional instability.

- They can lead to feelings of frustration, anger and dissatisfaction with the relationship.

- Decreased self-esteem and self-worth as you or your spouse feel devalued or unheard.

- You or your spouse can experience mental exhaustion from the constant cycle of conflict and power struggles.

- Prioritizing power struggles over personal well-being undermines self-care and individual growth.

20.5 Diminished Relationship Satisfaction:

Power Struggles negatively impact overall relationship satisfaction and happiness.

When the focus is on asserting power rather than building a loving and supportive relationship, you and your spouse will suffer.

Practice these **KEYS**:

- Reduced satisfaction as you or your spouse may feel unfulfilled and emotionally disconnected.

- The relationship becomes a source of stress and unhappiness rather than a source of comfort and joy.

- Long-term relationship dissatisfaction can lead to increased risk of separation or divorce.

20.6 Impact on Children and Family Dynamics:

Power Struggles within a marriage can have a profound impact on children and the overall family dynamic. Children are sensitive to the conflict and tension between their parents and it can influence their own emotional well-being and future relationships.

Practice these **KEYS**:

- Children may experience heightened anxiety, insecurity and confusion when exposed to constant power struggles.

- Children learn from observing their parents' interactions and may adopt similar patterns in their own relationships.

- By avoiding power struggles, you model healthy conflict resolution and promote a positive family dynamic.

20.7 Impaired Problem-Solving and Decision-Making:

Power Struggles hinder effective problem-solving and decision-making within a marriage. When you or your spouse are focused on asserting power rather than finding mutually beneficial solutions, important issues go unresolved.

Practice these **KEYS**:

- Inability to reach compromises and make decisions that serve the best interests of both you and your spouse.

- Important issues may be ignored or pushed aside, leading to long-term resentment and dissatisfaction.

- The lack of effective problem-solving skills can result in recurring conflicts and a stagnant relationship.

The effects of power struggles in your marriage are far-reaching and detrimental to both you and your spouse and the overall well-being of the relationship. Recognizing the erosion of trust and intimacy, breakdown in communication, emotional and mental distress, diminished relationship satisfaction, impact on children and family dynamics, and impaired problem-solving and decision-making can serve as a catalyst for change. By actively working towards a healthy and balanced partnership, characterized by open communication, mutual respect, and collaboration, you can break free from the destructive cycle of power struggles and create a loving and fulfilling relationship. Remember, prioritizing love, understanding, and empathy over power will contribute to the growth and happiness of both you and your spouse.

Chapter 21
Your Past, Our Future

*"Learn from your past, apply it in the present and
live the life you were meant to live."*

The past experiences, upbringing, and individual
histories of both you and your spouse play a significant role in shaping the dynamics and trajec-
tory of a marriage. While the past can bring challenges
and potential conflicts, it also holds the potential for
growth, understanding and deep connection. In this
chapter, we will explore how the past can both impact
and benefit the future of a married couple.

21.1 Understanding Each Other's Past:

Reflecting on your individual pasts allows for a deeper
understanding and compassion toward each other. By
recognizing the influences of your upbringing, previous
relationships, and personal experiences, you can cultivate empathy and support.

Practice these **KEYS**:

- Sharing your past experiences allows your
  spouse to understand your motivations, fears
  and triggers.

- It provides an opportunity for empathy and
  compassion, as you gain insight into each other's
  journeys.

- Understanding each other's past fosters a sense of validation, acceptance and support.

21.2 Unpacking Baggage:

You and your spouse bring your own unique set of experiences, beliefs and emotional baggage into the marriage. These can range from childhood traumas to past relationships and cultural backgrounds.

Practice these **KEYS**:

- Past experiences can influence how you perceive and respond to certain triggers or conflicts in your marriage.

- Unresolved issues from the past can resurface and impact your emotional well-being and the overall dynamic of the marriage.

- Understanding and unpacking your individual baggage can lead to personal growth, empathy and healing.

21.3 Identifying Potential Triggers:

The past can serve as a source of insight into potential triggers and sensitive areas for you both. By recognizing and communicating these triggers, you can create a safe and supportive environment within your marriage.

Practice these **KEYS**:

- Awareness of past traumas or triggers allows you to approach difficult situations with sensitivity and care.

- Open communication about triggers helps to prevent unnecessary conflicts and misunderstandings.

- Acknowledging triggers fosters an environment of respect and empathy, minimizing the negative impact of past wounds.

21.4 Learning from Mistakes:

Past mistakes, whether in relationships or personal choices, provide valuable lessons that can inform and guide your future as a couple. Embracing the lessons learned can help you avoid similar pitfalls and make informed decisions together.

Practice these **KEYS**:

- Reflecting on past mistakes fosters personal growth and maturity.

- Sharing and discussing past errors with your spouse promotes open and honest communication.

- Learning from mistakes as a couple strengthens your commitment to making healthier choices in the future.

21.5 Breaking Unhealthy Patterns:

Examining the past will enable you and your spouse to identify and break unhealthy patterns that may have been carried forward into the relationship. By actively working together, you can overcome destructive behaviors and create healthier dynamics.

Practice these **KEYS**:

- Recognizing negative patterns from the past empowers you to make conscious choices for positive change.

- By addressing and resolving past issues, you can prevent their recurrence and create a healthier future.

- Breaking unhealthy patterns fosters personal growth and allows the relationship to flourish in a more positive direction.

21.6 Cultural and Family Backgrounds:

Your cultural and family backgrounds shape your values, traditions and perspectives on various aspects of life. Recognizing and embracing these differences can enrich your relationship and provide opportunities for growth and learning.

Practice these **KEYS**:

- Cultural backgrounds offer unique perspectives and traditions that can be celebrated and integrated into your marriage.

- Understanding each other's family dynamics and traditions fosters empathy and connection.

- Blending different cultural backgrounds can create a rich and diverse tapestry in your relationship.

21.7 Establishing Shared Goals and Visions:

While the past can shape your future as a couple, it is important to establish shared goals and visions that reflect your collective aspirations. Embracing shared values, strengths and positive experiences fosters a sense of unity and shared purpose.

Practice these **KEYS**:

*   Incorporating lessons from the past into shared goals promotes unity and a sense of purpose.

*   Creating a shared vision allows you to navigate challenges and make decisions that are in alignment with your collective values.

*   A shared future provides a sense of direction and motivation, enhancing your bond as a couple.

21.8 Unveiling New Possibilities:

Embracing the past can unlock new possibilities and potentials within your marriage. By exploring and integrating each other's pasts, you can discover uncharted territories and shared dreams.

Practice these **KEYS**:

*   The past can inspire new passions, hobbies, and shared interests that bring excitement and joy to the relationship.

*   Learning from each other's past successes and failures expands the realm of possibilities for personal and joint growth.

*   Embracing the past opens up doors to unexpected adventures and opportunities for a fulfilling future together.

The past, with its complexities and experiences has the power to shape and influence the future of a married couple. By understanding and empathizing with each other's pasts, identifying triggers, breaking unhealthy patterns, building on strengths and shared values and unveiling new possibilities, you can create a future characterized by growth, understanding and a deep sense of connection. Embrace the lessons and wisdom gained from the past and embark on a journey of continuous growth and mutual support. Remember, your past can serve as a powerful catalyst for a fulfilling and meaningful future together. So embrace the opportunity to support each other's growth, celebrate your uniqueness, and create a future filled with love, resilience and shared purpose.